Gardening

Teaching Tips

Orange Level 6

This book focuses on the phonemes **/o_e/oe/**.

Before Reading

- Discuss the title. Ask readers what they think the book will be about. Have them briefly explain why.
- Ask readers to say the name of each object on page 3. Which ones end in o_e? What letters and sounds do the names of the other objects end in?

Read the Book

- Encourage readers to break down unfamiliar words into units of sound. Then, ask them to string the sounds together to create the words.
- Urge readers to point out when the focused phonics phonemes appear in the text.

After Reading

- Encourage children to reread the book independently or with a friend.
- Ask readers to name other words with /o_e/ or /oe/ phonemes. On a separate sheet of paper, have them write the words out.

© 2024 Booklife Publishing
This edition is published by arrangement with Booklife Publishing.

North American adaptations © 2024 Jump!
5357 Penn Avenue South
Minneapolis, MN 55419
www.jumplibrary.com

Decodables by Jump! are published by Jump! Library.
All rights reserved. No part of this book may be reproduced in any form without written permission from the publisher.

Library of Congress Cataloging-in-Publication Data is available at www.loc.gov or upon request from the publisher.

ISBN: 979-8-88996-858-0 (hardcover)
ISBN: 979-8-88996-859-7 (paperback)
ISBN: 979-8-88996-860-3 (ebook)

Photo Credits

Images are courtesy of Shutterstock.com. With thanks to Getty Images, Thinkstock Photo and iStockphoto. Cover – Pixel-Shot. 2–3 – LesPalenik, Tarzhanova, Svetlana Serebryakova, VIEWVEAR, PROFFIPhoto, BCFC, khunkornStudio, ruzanna. 4–5 – michaeljung, Serhii Bobyk. 6–7 – amedeoemaja, Aleksandr Malivuk. 8–9 – Lost_in_the_Midwest, Jon Rehg. 10–11 – Artith chotitayangkoon, Virrage Images. 12–13 – VH-studio, Miguel Angel RM, CandyRetriever. 14–15 – dasytnik, Sentelia. 16 – Shutterstock.

Which of these objects have o_e in their name?

Gardening is a big job. Gardeners need to make sure that all the plants in a garden are looked after.

Gardeners may travel to big public gardens to do their jobs. Some may travel to little gardens at peoples' homes.

When it is hot, gardeners check that each plant gets the right amount of water. They may get out a hose or a watering can to help.

It is best for gardeners to spray close to the stem. This way, water goes right to the roots.

Some gardens have a problem with weeds and stones. They can choke the plants that are supposed to be growing there.

Gardeners can use a hoe to help them pull up weeds in the soil. Some hoes have a long pole so that people do not have to stoop as low.

If a garden has grass, it will need to be mowed. Flat gardens are better to cut. Cutting on a slope can be hard.

Gardeners need to be careful so that they do not get hurt. They cannot let their toes near the mower's blade.

Blade

Gardeners check that plants are not sick. If they are, gardeners work to make those plants better.

Some plants get attacked by bugs. Gardeners might have to spray them to keep the bugs off.

Bugs on a rose

Gardeners do not just look after adult plants. They may plant new ones too. First, they poke a hole in some soil.

Then, they drop a seed in the hole and get it wet. They let the pot sit in the sunlight. Soon, a new plant springs up!

Can you name the missing letters for each word?

m__l__

t____

her____s